SandCastle

Let's Go!

LET'S GO

BY

CAR

ANDERS HANSON

Consulting Editor, Diane Craig, M.A./Reading Specialist

ABDO Publishing Company

Published by ABDO Publishing Company, 8000 West 78th Street, Edina, MN 55439.

Copyright © 2008 by Abdo Consulting Group, Inc. International copyrights reserved in all countries. No part of this book may be reproduced in any form without written permission from the publisher. SandCastle™ is a trademark and logo of ABDO Publishing Company.

Printed in the United States.

Editor: Pam Price
Curriculum Coordinator: Nancy Tuminelly
Cover and Interior Design and Production: Mighty Media
Photo Credits: Shutterstock, Stockbyte

Library of Congress Cataloging-in-Publication Data

Hanson, Anders, 1980-
  Let's go by car / Anders Hanson.
    p. cm. -- (Let's go!)
  ISBN 978-1-59928-897-0
  1. Automobiles--Juvenile literature. 2. Automobile travel--Juvenile literature. I. Title.

TL147.H26 2008
629.2--dc22

                                                                2007006420

SandCastle™ Level: Transitional

SandCastle™ books are created by a team of professional educators, reading specialists, and content developers around five essential components—phonemic awareness, phonics, vocabulary, text comprehension, and fluency—to assist young readers as they develop reading skills and increase their general knowledge. All books are written, reviewed, and leveled for guided reading, early intervention reading, and Accelerated Reader® programs for use in shared, guided, and independent reading and writing activities to support a balanced approach to literacy instruction. The SandCastle™ series has four levels that correspond to early literacy development. The levels are provided to help teachers and parents select appropriate books for young readers.

Emerging Readers
(no flags)

Beginning Readers
(1 flag)

Transitional Readers
(2 flags)

Fluent Readers
(3 flags)

SandCastle™ would like to hear from you. Please send us your comments or questions.

sandcastle@abdopublishing.com

A car has four wheels and an engine. Cars travel on roads and carry just a few people.

An engine gives a car power.

5

In some cars, a stick shift controls gears in the engine.

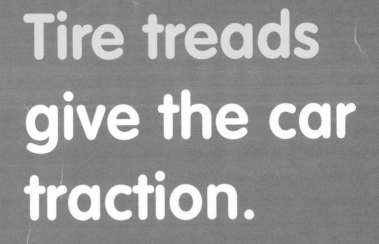

Tire treads give the car traction.

The speed of the car is shown on the speedometer.

Steve and
his sister are
taking a trip to
see their aunt.

Amy likes to help wash her mom's car.

Melinda sleeps easily in the car.

Madison's parents always make sure her seat belt and car seat are secure.

WHAT DO YOU DO IN A CAR?

WHERE DO YOU GO?

TYPES OF CARS

convertible

compact car

hatchback

sedan

sports car

station wagon

John Evans of England holds a world record for balancing a car on his head for 33 seconds. The car weighed 352 pounds.

In 1918, more than half of the cars in America were Model T Fords.

The first cars were steered with a lever instead of a steering wheel.

GLOSSARY

compact – a car that is smaller than a standard car.

convertible – having a top that can be lowered or removed.

gear – a wheel with bumps on it.

hatchback – a car with a door on the back that lifts upward.

sedan – a car that has front and back seats and holds four or more people.

traction – the friction that helps a tire grip the road.

To see a complete list of SandCastle™ books and other nonfiction titles from ABDO Publishing Company, visit **www.abdopublishing.com**.

8000 West 78th Street, Edina, MN 55439 • 800-800-1312 • 952-831-1632 fax